Hints and Allegations

Hints and Allegations

Amanda J. Bradley

The New York Quarterly Foundation, Inc.
New York, New York

NYQ Books™ is an imprint of The New York Quarterly Foundation, Inc.

The New York Quarterly Foundation, Inc.
P. O. Box 2015
Old Chelsea Station
New York, NY 10113

www.nyqbooks.org

Copyright © 2009 by Amanda J. Bradley

All rights reserved. No part of this book may be used or reproduced in any manner whatsoever without written permission of the author. This book is a work of fiction. Any references to historical events, real people or real locales are used fictitiously. Other names, characters, places, and incidents are products of the author's imagination, and any resemblance to actual events or locales or persons, living or dead, is entirely coincidental.

First Edition

Set in New Baskerville

Layout and Design by Raymond P. Hammond
Cover Illustration by Eric Bradley

Library of Congress Control Number: 2009933335

ISBN: 978-1-935520-07-8

Hints and Allegations

Acknowledgments

Grateful acknowledgment is made to the editors of the following journals in which these poems first appeared: "Seed," *The Toronto Quarterly;* "Insomnia," *decomP magazinE;* "Unscathed," *Barefoot Muse;* "Prostration," "The Desert," "Listen," "Every Rose," *The New York Quarterly;* "Fantasy," *Mad Poets Review;* "Listen," *Soul Fountain;* "The Desert," *Dufus;* "A Gift," *Pennine Ink;* "A Gift," *Gentle Reader;* "This Intuition," *Zillah;* "Her Quilt," *Poetry Bay;* "Hair and Nails," *Poetic Hours;* "A Gift," "Hair and Nails," *Down in the Dirt.*

for my grandmother
Betty Pearcy

Contents

I. Disturbance

The Following	15
Alert	16
Facing	17
Beneath	18
Among You	19
Apartment Building 3:00 A.M.	20
Fantasy	22
Choreography	23
Ambivalence	24
Suspended in Disbelief	25
Shades of Gray	26
Desert	27
Insomnia	28
Bittersweet	29
Choice	30
O TRY 2	31
Plates	32
Every Rose	33
WELL DUH	34
Thought	35
Revisiting El Dorado, Arkansas	36
Prostration	38
Who Do I Think You Are	39
Sound and Sense	40
Surface	41

Unscathed	42
Cipher	44
Sticks and Stones	46
Chasing Tails	47

II. Equilibrium

This Intuition	51
Her Quilt	52
Listen	54
Stone	55
Seed	56
Window	57
Agnostic	58
A Gift	59
And It Was So…	60
Hair and Nails	62
Freedom	63
Seeing Clearly	64
Appearances	65
Suits of Woe	66
Who's There	67
What It Must Be Like as a Logical Thinker	68
Turn	70
Anticipation	71
Any One	72

Much Madness is divinest Sense—
To a discerning Eye—
Much Sense—the starkest Madness—
'Tis the Majority
In this, as All, prevail—
Assent—and you are sane—
Demur—you're straightway dangerous—
And handled with a Chain—

    Emily Dickinson
    Poem 435

Perhaps a lunatic was simply a minority of one.

    George Orwell
    1984

Nobody's right if everybody's wrong.

    Stephen Stills
    Buffalo Springfield
    "For What It's Worth"

Disturbance

The Following

    The following will
           importune you
beg of you
           questions you'd like to know
   real
living answers to

    The following will
           make you wonder
why you never
         feel the
  push
until you're over the wall

    The following will
           leave in ruins
the façade, the
  line
between here and there
           where only you know

    The following will
           render meaningless
the following, will
  you
forgive it that, will
you follow?

Alert

I am alert because alerted.
What is there to do
with this inertia?
Had I said, "I know,"
would you have thought
me arrogant
Me Jane?
I never notify authorities.
It is always someone else.
Most of us get by with
So much
So little.
I want to spill it all—
the milk, the beans.
I hear the natural wisdom
of language,
words pointing wildly in
poignant directions.
We are not conscious enough
to have created it. It is
far too brutal, too wise.
We doublespeak always,
attempting to step, but
slipping and slipping and slipping,
silently bared but
safely barred as well.
Do not worry.
Babble on.
Know that you should hear.
Remain bold if embarrassed.
I will not tell the authorities.
I am not counting.
Who are they to me
but pricklers—mindless,
spurring, sparring masters.

Facing

Nothing's wrong with nonsense
except the giving in
the giving over
the sneaking, sinking under
getting nowhere.
This business of affairs
had and not had
weighs one down—
the dancing around
thinking there's plenty of time
from we meet at last
to forget me not.
I have been facing
the blank, black eye
of the pigeons strutting
on the tar of the roof over.
It is what I was seeking
if anything at all.

Beneath

Awful laughter
Because silence is vicious
Odd, bastard tears that do not redeem
But humiliate
A harrowing, pulsing cunt
Who can control the rage of blood
The bastard tears, the hell of laughter
Afraid to step outside
As ravaged as a tree in a storm
And this is life, this body
That cannot be stopped

Among You

You cannot force me
to believe their lies—
the paradox.
Are you even trying?
I hear only silence
and terrible hints.
I walk among you a ghost
and yet I walk.
You hear my babble,
which makes me other-wise
invisible.
I cannot connect
yesterday to today to tomorrow.
I am
out of time.
But I am not alone
when I choose not to be
I can lie
with the other whores.
We are a ruby red lot.
Who can save me from
where I've landed—
in the shadows of my own
private, paltry apocalypse.

Apartment Building 3:00 A.M.

A tumbler has fallen on its side
And remains there,
Steadied somehow,
Next to an empty pizza box.
Static blares from the TV,
As the old man sprawls on
His ancient couch that hasn't been
Vacuumed in this era of his life.

A spooning young couple lies
Sated and sleeping,
Naked under crisp sheets.
They are blissfully poor
With plans for their future
Which may or may not come
To fruition, but they now believe
That all seeds land on fertile ground.

A microwaved frozen dinner
Lies cold and unfinished on a tv tray.
Surrounded by framed pictures,
Waiting for pills to kill arthritic pain,
In a pink terry cloth robe with a sash,
The elderly woman remembers the
Last time her daughters visited
With a clouded mind.

Too aware of his loneliness to sleep
Tonight, still watching porn in his
Boxers, socks, undershirt, the aging
Man leaves half-smoked cigarettes
In the ashtrays, absentmindedly
Putting them out one after another.
His determined vision of happiness is
A girl that beautiful, that unselfish.

The kids are tucked in bed, and
The dishes were done by hand
With detergent containing aloe.
The single mother finally finds
Spare moments to read, her hobby.
Her favorites are mystery novels,
Full of excitement and intrigue.
She can always guess the ending.

Fantasy

a simple idea
virtual, unreal
fed daily through
introspection
grows exciting
actual, lived
eventually
a wall erects
around it
with cracks
too small
to see through,
impenetrable,
Reality

Choreography

Our dance is synchronized
as at a formal ball.
Part of a dark masquerade,
we are attuned.
The end carries whispers
through our numbers
only for us
to realize that we interrupt
the music.
And so we fall to silence.
This dance feels natural;
we rarely stumble.
We watch each other's eyes,
nod knowingly
for a peculiar reason
as we pass one another,
holding fast to the dance
by light fingertips.

Ambivalence

Catapulted into gray dreams,
I can no longer differentiate
Between life and death,
Truth and lie, right and wrong.
Is this the solipsism
I once laughed at?
If it must be this way,
Put me on a stretcher.
Anesthetize me for good.
I know I am a heavy load.
Borrow pall bearers.
Your graciousness
Bares me, leaves me indebted.
I do not want to owe you.
So stash me away;
Do what you do with my likes.
Now that I fear this fight
Will never end, anesthetize me.
For all I know
You are vessels of God,
Accidentally flashing my life
Before me with your words.
It is a mean love
In my imperfect eyes.

Suspended in Disbelief

No cause for confusion
Yet there it is
Maker of bad moods
Distiller of contradictions

I draw a bath
Crawl into hot water
Pull the plug
Slow voluble streams
Drain at my feet
Each moment I better
Feel my weight
I momentarily stay
Watching steam lift from my knees
Listening to bubbles crackle
Soaking in the tub's heat

Next, I will
Don Chinese slippers
Wish for a sombrero
Whisper aloud

Shades of Gray

My creaturely attention span dictates
today I don't care,
yet some vague obligation to participate remains.
Out the window, down on the street
two boys strike each other with sticks.
They don't look up.

I walk, and accidental wisdoms seem to slip
through innocent winds. I feel myself age,
and I am glad. Two women pass with canes
in silent communion, hunched over. I search
their serene eyes, struggling for gratitude.

Desert

I thought I'd desire you as long
as the desert desires a drink
only to realize that deserts don't.
They are as quenched as the rainforests.
Deserts are places for temptations,
for our ancient recollections.
Their winds erode permanence;
they swallow footprints,
require but sparse fulfillment,
will show you a mirage
because you are weak: so much water.
I became a desert soul
thinking I could desire you so long,
losing my footprints in the sand,
searching for an oasis.
I am no longer thirsty.
I am arid.
At night, I will chill them to the bone.
I will hide them in my vast, tiny sands.

Insomnia

Night-washed thoughts wander
crevices of skeletal ideas.
We're bare bones here.
Our waking dream appears omniscient,
feels tangible when it's late.
God surely exists at night.
Prowling dreamscapes,
it all seems more likely in the dark.
Loosened imagination paints
the dark with designs and desires.
Don't pick *my* lock.
Reflections recall the negatively-tinged,
as if the moon's magnetism
pulled vast secrets from within—
secrets we did not realize we were keeping,
secrets that expand
in the wild of night's embrace.

Bittersweet

The smoke centers me
I can feel my self
I can know I am
Rotting, chemicals
In my brain adjusting
With each puff, each breath
I finally know I will not
Be here forever because
My shoes wore out and
My collarbone broke and
I bit my tongue and
I find that comforting.

Choice

Bogart my life.
See what I'll do.
Involve people.
Call it art.
Call it community.
Call it a farce.
Get famous.
Lie to my face.
Cajole
    Threaten
        Humiliate
Me.
Think you are better.
Think you love me,
if you must.

O TRY 2

what the thieves took
what silenced you
what conviction I lack
what postmodern is
why you let me know
why you think it's funny
why I think you're arrogant
why we'll never
when I'm reached
when it's over
when we die

Plates

WIMP
ADJUST
THE FRAZ
I ARGU 2
WRITE ON
LOVEDREW
FOUR MGS
WELL DUH
I VU ALL
SHAVER
GOLD DIGGER
HOT SPOT
REPENT 2
GAVE IN
UP ON IT
GET SMWHR
B READY
B LUCID 2
SWEET 36
NY MAGIC 2
BIGUP2BK
RAYNANCY
JET RIG
JUHSTUS
POET 1850
ANGRY 2
FAR MORE

Every Rose

I can't.
I can't forgive you.
I won't.
I won't do that.
I was.
I was right to run.

I wish.
I wish you hadn't.
I hope.
I hope you're happy.
I will.
I will move on.

I think you are…
a spider web glistening with dew
a prickle on the back of my neck
another difficult day to live through
a thought I intentionally subvert
a feeling I don't want to have

You make me
a minus sign
a Mona Lisa
a thorn

WELL DUH

Though you always tout
bucking the system,
you must realize
that you *are* my system.
So I have to buck you.

Thought

Minnows dodge through my mind's muddy pool.
They collide and gnaw each other's gills,
dying, growing, swimming, circling, circling.
They mate and bear new thoughts to join
the confused, repressed mass,
struggling to reach the surface and evolve.

Revisiting El Dorado, Arkansas

Passing through Arkansas, I recall
tiptoeing over tufts of hair, wrenched
from heads in fights between classes.
They all remained loyal
to their circles: white and rich
and black and poor. The lunchroom,
at a particularly integrated school, showed
the split.

I remember confederate flags
tacked up on walls of friends' bedrooms,
confederate flags in truck windows, on bumpers,
belonging to smart people. Friends said they grew up
young—learning to drink at eight, drive at nine.
Everyone knew everyone in town,
and they had all told each other's stories
many times.

Thank God for Angela—the outcast, the misfit,
the girl with a funny accent who dressed
like a man. She was lucky she's so pretty.
Once, as we tooled around the countryside
in August in her purple MG convertible,
our long blond hairs mingling in the wind,
we started singing the same Beatles song
at the same second.

It caused a stir when we moved to El Dorado;
the town welcomed us with lemonade,
Tom Collins, and southern hospitality.
Slowly, close-mouthed, we learned the legends.
The one I never forgot was the one about
the neighbor's son who might have lynched
a black man in my lifetime, not long before
he went to law school.

Prostration

You are a natural leader, requiring rank and file
beneath you. This impressed me, drew me to you
like so many of your peons, your minions.
"Stoic," "statuesque": these words you used to describe me
as I sat blithely on the couch enjoying the furor
I was driving you into with my blank face, smoking,
secretly relishing the anticipation of the inevitable
sexual attack in which you would, with your
knowing hands, tongue, body pressure just the right
points, making me want to surrender, finally,
to your will. You wanted me to be more
of a girl, fawning, cuddling, quietly in awe of you,
a demi-god in your own mind, haunted by demons.
I was paralyzed, watching the world's dance, everything
operating in unison in my eyes. We were torturing,
saving one another, from the depths of
our separate nervous breakdowns. So we rose
and sank into more curious sex and more dangerous
fights. What if the bullet had shot through my stomach,
in that one moment of my daring you, if I hadn't broken
the lock on the bathroom door, to find you hanging,
naked, of course, and strung up symbolically with
a tie my grandmother had given you – because you
felt the outside world pulling me back to a semblance of sanity,
to something akin to normalcy, away from our tortuous,
loving, deathly circle of two, holding hands as we
skipped, terrified and merry, utterly without irony,
into hell on earth, saved only by our own passions.

Who Do I Think You Are

I so wanted to be what you wanted
me to be. You said, "I bet you sleep nude."
And I did. In my tiny, shared dorm room,
I abandoned comfortable tee shirt
and flannels for you, simply one
of many changes I would make to prove
myself worthy, to prove you right.
We all want to be right,
but we've got different reasons for that.
You must think it's the principle
of the thing. The thing is
I've become ugly in your hands, your mind,
your eyes, even—it's your doing,
my undoing, and you walk blithely
away to a life I'll never have
because of you, your interference,
your clouding of my already faulty
judgment. You broke your toy
and, like a little bully boy, walked
away, acting as if you didn't.
Denial is your weapon. I am fistless.
My tears are my only defense, and you
never see me shed them. What
is clearly resentment, hatred, you might,
with all your glorified, artful theorizing,
consider love at its most pure, its finest,
but I'll know, I'll know, I'll know.

Sound and Sense

caught in the sound
lost in the sense
that words run together
hand in hand across
the playground of the page
of pentacles turns up
on my table as if
at my door, knocking
down the suitors and the
salesmen—wait—
that doesn't happen any more
than trusting strangers
to not say hello because
we are caught in the
sound lost in the sense

Surface

Passing mirrors, we glance or stare.
Turning hands from back to palm,
we see skin, surface.
Young, reflections fascinate,
and the dexterity of hands.
Growing old is different.

We quietly cry out from within
the hole we dig. Paralysis occurs.
Our hands can no longer hold the pick.
Ultimately, there is no more need
to dig, for who can reach us
here beneath the surface.

Unscathed

I have decided I do not want to have a baby.
Maybe I can appease my instincts and plant a garden
Instead. Don't we all have an urge to create?
Children carry through them their memories
Of you; I suppose I will plant and write.
There are many ways to escape mortality.

The most common, rampant deceit of mortality
Is the phenomenal event of having a baby,
Bloody and wailing for breast milk. Do words we write
Cry as loudly? Do azaleas and thyme in a garden
Recognize your voice, your hands, hold memories,
Allow you to whisper stories to their children they create?

Children use imagination, crayons, games to create.
Some of them, keep in mind, have no chance to trick mortality.
Those live on, heavy in the breasts, the memories
Of their families. That is why I cannot have a baby.
I am a coward full of compassion who will garden.
Words can fail; they cannot feel. I will write.

It is a labor of love, a numinous challenge, to write.
The offspring of images, events, ideas you create
Form a lush, intricate, vining, veiny garden
That lets you make believe you outwit mortality.
A writer has an enormous head, like a baby
Tearing through a vagina: both makers of original memories.

Our heads are full. Life is the maker of memories.
We want to record, to capture retreating moments, to write.
Mothers have written their stories of having a baby.
It is suffering, ecstasy, responsibility, fear to create,
To worry for all aspects of another's life, mortality.
Together, mothers and children can plant a messy garden.

But I will cultivate an elegant, carefully planned garden.
Why not? We are all walking bundles of memories.
We must seize all opportunities to wonder at our mortality.
We are all damaged. Look at what we write,
Why we try to improve each generation, to create
A child who will walk unharmed, the perfect baby.

In our myths, our mortality began in a luxuriant garden.
Our maker's very first baby is hidden in our memories.
I wish I could write the unscathed into existence, to truly create.

Cipher

You come at me from all sides
like shrapnel:

"She thinks she's just going to blast through here."
"I liked her in the beginning."
"I thought she was supposed to be good looking."
"Nothing's too good for *you*."
"We have no choice."

My mother is losing sleep.
I never know why.
Everything of substance to me
is darkened.
I am an entrance
to a cave blocked by a stone.

Lots of people
have it harder than me—
millions, maybe
billions.

I just wanted to muddle
through, like we do
"Who wants to lead a mediocre life?"

It's the relentlessness that gets me
and the new uses of language
and the fact that I can't stop talking
and thinking about this
and the push, the pull,
the this way, the that way.

Stop defining me, I want to say.
You negate me.

"You don't like commercials, do you?
They give *me* ideas."

Sticks and Stones

the world is not round
it is all sharp edges
now we know
a pregnant woman
was killed
so was another
the pendulum swings
invention, mission drive
are double edged
now we know
we round ones have ended
with a great responsibility
we must prove the earth
is a lollipop
that can be licked away
by a forked tongue

Chasing Tails

Dribble, Drabble
Drivel, gavel
Watch the mystery unravel
Squarely now, I am in my
New place, just having
Escaped
Some scaffold
You know those moments
Sometimes years
Lives depending
Slip on gravel and yet travel
Forward, always forward
We might as well be marching
Even chasing tails
Aye, there's the rub a dub dub
Attractions lead to
Atomic misunderstandings
It's an old story
Our dribbling
Our scribbling
We are the worms that eat us
When cut in half, we
Regenerate
And there we are—
Chopped in two, ready to crawl
In our doubled consciousness
Through more mysteries
Let me slither through your
Sockets, my new love
Perhaps death will seem more
Deliberate.

Equilibrium

This Intuition

Inside memory, yet
Still, presently aware:
One grows accustomed to it.
It spells time backwards.
See the coincidence
Requiring a subject
To objectively send time's line
Swerving
To split the atom, the infinitive,
To make time radiate.
It mimics
The course of an electron
Whose destination can be measured,
Predicted,
Whose path pressures.

Her Quilt

Her presence disturbs any scene.
She wills it to, striding through the door.
Otherwise she would not be here, outside her rooms.
They either flock or gossip. She is Mae West.
She beats them to the punch,
Coaxes them inside out; they are her fools.
Perhaps late tonight or in the morning light
She will become Medusa.
She desires resistance; they are pliable.
Why can no one guess her fantasy?
I will never tell this secret.
They do not deserve to know.

These are her rooms—all colorful, patterned cloth,
Rich half-burnt candles, meticulously made bed,
Ordered books, black dishes, orange teapot, spiced teas
And potpourris, old photos of despised family.
She says she cannot love. The idea is shocking
Like her hoop earrings, incompatible somehow
With her long hair and large breasts.
She believes in nothing and yet reads Russian
Fortune cards. She ferociously fears death—
Her extinguished individuality,
And yet it means nothing to her—to live, to die.

Her rejection of all abstract comforts
Is a carefully woven quilt that covers me
In the cold crowd of platitudes that surround me.
It is fabricated, but she would point out
That all things are. I like this fabrication.
It is intricate and bold. I want her
Meaninglessness, her cold, mean philosophy.
She has suffered loss. She is a frightened girl.
She takes on the responsibility like a queen
Hiding behind her staff.
She has killed her father
And hidden the body.

Listen

We breed an urge
to tell each other something
in systems we constitute.
We want to ease a burdened
conscious.
We confess and lie,
let language define,
identify.
What of the power inherent
in the untold,
what of the nature resistant
to our words.
Our knowledge alters
when we offer
recognition.
Listen to what we are
uttering.

Stone

Your memory is a statue
Erected as a reminder
Weathered as time passes
Detailed, but inaccurate
Chiseled slowly into existence
Lifeless

Seed

Death is an unjust idea, and I am against it.
The licking flame refuses to extinguish.
I still dream and always wake.
Barely able to imagine a single final thing, alive,
I hum. I change. I feel. I am aware.
Monsoons cannot convince me, nor
earthquakes, nor cancer, so energetic
are they, such value do they import
into this second and this and this.
In my mind, death is a seed buried deep—
a mysterious, dormant seed planted at birth,
destined to grow in the unknown.

Window

There is, in the sweet, close cross
of one life with another
something to absorb desire
something free in the impression
of shared memories
something shocking us into seeing
this could be the last
night this year
we leave the window open.

Agnostic

A robotically rational mind might think once
through the dilemma of obsolescence
before its explicit inevitability became clear
and no longer worth considering. But we—
we humans prove so irrational that artificial
intelligence has more genuine sense.
We can organize ones and zeros to think
sanely, so why insist on bemoaning our demise,
beating our heads up against the facts
until our addled brains conjure heavens.
We apparently need motivation to feed
and educate the poor. We, perversely, need
rewards—an after life so awesome that it is
beyond our ken. So little capacity to think
thoughts deep and wide as God, so little
capacity to know what happens when we die,
so many unknowns, why not spend ourselves
creating a better here and now for one and all.
And for that, when I have one, my God is
more understanding, more rational than
the God of vengeance and lives after deaths.

A Gift

You gave me a fishbowl.
You watched as I oohed,
as I pressed my face nearly flush
with the transparent surface.
One inch
between my cornea and the glass,
as if I could see more clearly
so close,
a unique perspective expanded.
From there, I could watch
water undulating,
the curve of the line,
the surface and the depth,
the textured patterns of the gills,
the fish awfully breathing
under water,
smoothly swimming into parts of the bowl
where space distorted
as I watched the fish become
enormous
in just seconds.

And It Was So...

We used to capture fireflies,
put them in a jar with holes in the lid.
In my memory,
those fireflies were
blue and pink and yellow-green.
At twenty-five, I finally noticed
a field of all yellow-green
fireflies. I realized
I had deceived myself
for nearly two decades.

And it was so...
Such ferocity, such exactitude,
such certainty of vision,
such decision
in calculations behind
human brain, serpent fang,
elephant trunk,
space,
sea.
To create variety and similarity,
growth and decay,
suffering and bliss,
knowledge and ignorance,
beginnings and ends...
To conjure one's own
apparentness and invisibility,
presence and absence,
omniscience and silence,
ubiquity and inertia...
To embody energy...

And it was so…
Such fragility, such humility,
such clarity of sentience,
such transparence
in existing within
colorful world, individual mind,
solid body,
language,
time.
To experience meaning and futility,
complexity and simplicity,
power and weakness,
solemnity and playfulness,
belief and doubt…
To sense one's own
time is measured
in some cosmic hourglass
flipped in another era
that is also now
To embody energy…

A friend and I were at the beach
when I was twelve, appalled
that the horseshoe crabs
had washed up to the shore.
Certain they would die there,
we carefully lifted as many as
we could, dragging them
back to sea one by one.
I no longer remember
my friend's name.

Hair and Nails

The tidal wave gathers
at sea.
Green grass waits
for spring.
Milk curdles
in the infant's stomach.
Do eyes really pop?
The dead leaf
dangles.
Enormous glaciers
push.
Distended bellies
line dirt streets.
Do cages really rattle?

Freedom

Knowing you are yourself
as impermanent as all things
Having forgiven all people
their trespasses
on your spirit,
your damned feet
Laughing
Wearing a silky red scarf
Walking an unpredictable path
Knowing you are yourself
as eternal and expendable
as the whole lot of them
The mystery of
accepting evanescence
A crocus in the snow
The feel of birch
Rushing water
The ground
for now
beneath your feet

Seeing Clearly

pass out in severe pain
walk on bed of coals
broken eggshells
brick red crayon in child's hand
sky blue for water on feet
we are drawn
stepping into hazy Atlantic
jellyfish
no crayon for transparent
salmon pink stinging tendrils
swimming back to shore unaware
of developing welts
until on sand; one fish, two fish
out of water
impressionist sand for accuracy
beige, tan, lemon yellow sun
dishwater blonde
head in the clouds
in the air
dizzy, proud, in pain
pass out all the same
different strokes
who knows what happens

Appearances

Just like hearing a baby's cry
Sent us running over barbed
Wire fences, through prickly weeds
Only to find an unhappy cat
And lose interest

Just like a sunrise and a sunset
Look identical except that one
Is fated to the east, one to the west
You know neither can be sufficiently
Painted or described

Just like I could be convinced
That no one has green eyes
When you, my dear love, so clearly do
So much is altered by revisions,
By tricks of thought, by our inadequacy,

By appearances

Suits of Woe

> *But I have that within which passes show,*
> *These are but the trappings and the suits of woe.*
> Hamlet, Act I, Scene 2, ll. 85-86

Oscillation from faith to doubt redoubled
Silly to debate
We all wear that old hat
But we are free to know not "seems"
Sure we are
Why pour only half the glass

What goes on inside forces
Social order molds a new unconscious
Nothing archaic about today's brain
No one is more individual than us
Lovingly tracing our fingers through sand
Ruefully tromping home against the tide

My faith is thick with history
My doubt grays and humbles like hair
Some inchoate thing has it in for us
But only in time, in time only, perhaps
We are clap-trapped in these liminalities
Learning to be, we begin to know

Who's There

Hold at arm's length where I am held cradled there, here, what year
Necessary, secrets are sexy. Growing old, growing aware
of what was always there: who created who created who created who
Trust sublime, tainted. There are too many of me. I am. I am.
We wear blind. We look different. To learn, to seek, to remain.
Experiments are better than judgments are worse than ignorance
Says who says who says who says. Knock.

What It Must Be Like as a Logical Thinker

It must be hot fudge sundaes, puppies with big feet
to think logically, rationally, with purpose and direction.
It must be an extra hour of sleep, Easter hats on girls,
a well done evening of Shakespeare. It's difficult
to imagine not making such silly associations, such strange
correspondences between this small event and that,
between something inside me and something out.
For example, when I think a word as someone I don't know
on the train randomly says it aloud, I take notice of that
moment. I wonder about it. I wonder about that word,
the significance of that line of thought. Should I somehow
imprint this moment with meaning, should I perhaps
consider its importance? What does the mere coincidence
make me think now? Does that matter? I can not not.
I am not even eavesdropping, not intently, always more
lost in my own line of thought and yet hearing simultaneously.
When a child walking by, holding her mother's hand says
"Why does the alphabet go from a to z?" to let it make me
think of the alpha and the omega, of religion and zeal and
questioning and purpose, when a store clerk asks for $10.66
for merchandise, to think of the Norman Conquest and progress
and how history unfolds and God's possible hand in it all
or not. When you say "pie," I think "pi." When you say
something incidental, I make it resonate, and this can become
overwhelming. Perhaps some of why Randall Jarrell stepped
in front of the car, why Hart Crane jumped ship, why Sylvia
Plath left her head in the oven. Because when someone says
"jump," and you do not think, instinctually, "how high" but rather,
meditatively, "what makes you say that and more importantly why?"
you will get lost some afternoons, some evenings, some hours.

It's a comfort to think "what a cute child," "I might have exact change," "yes, pie," to stay rooted in a logical reality. But perhaps those of you who can manage such absence of abstraction in your thought processes, such precision of focus and such concern for what must be done next, perhaps you are simply not noticing.

Turn

Careful whispers still, take down my doubts,
murder them and sniff round the remains.
They'll reincarnate, something better, tamed
by mere suggestion, working out the faults.
The miracle workers teem and grow by days,
show each other, deliberate, how to live,
create together, sensible, how to give.
Scan the crowd for the knowing, steady gaze.

The need for crap like lies and fears and greed
dispelled by larger forces, apt concerns,
ruined in the wake of something right.
So those who cling to older ways take heed.
Your apocalypse is coming with the turn.
You too will be discovered in the night.

Anticipation

If we could first know where we are, and whither we are tending, we could then better judge what to do, and how to do it.
—Abraham Lincoln

...said the sign on the subway.
But, I thought, how boring
it would be if we knew
where and whither, how life
would be another endeavor entirely,
were our expectations so shallow
for the knowing. Anticipation,
discovery, awe, the process
of learning, of aging—perhaps
there is nothing to do and no way
to do it. Perhaps...
Milton could only imagine a heaven
of worshipping angels—all there is
without where and whither.
May we never know. May we
always wonder. May we remain.

Any One

> *And everyone who ever had a heart*
> *They wouldn't turn around and break it*
> *And anyone who ever played a part*
> *Wouldn't turn around and hate it*
>   —Lou Reed

I.

This experimental way of relating
attempts to approach truth
through a cold hard stare and a lack
of lies. Well…I suppose…
the central lie is large and corrodes
the rest of the experiment
in my view, like a rogue element
in an otherwise pristine Petri dish.
The extent of my scientific analysis
is subconscious. I imagine lab rats
don't care if we get anti-aging cream
and a cure for cancer out of it.
I don't blame them.
You could find a way to collaborate
that changes the face of Peace Studies
and I still would not forgive you.
Besides, if we've learned anything,
isn't it that truth can only be approached,
never reached…

II.

Suspicious of peace, of enlightenment,
I prove intractable. I will not be moved.
I am more of the suffering-is-necessary-
for-progress-and-art camp. Men, I read,
are more likely to be geniuses than women,
are more likely to be fuck-ups, too. I do
believe greatness can only be achieved
through suffering. I buy that hook, line,
and sinker. They go together like a bodhisattva
and Dharma, like the jazz greats and heroin,
like Schiele and poverty, like Plath and Hughes.
Enlightened people try to escape
what I embrace—suffering. Comfortable
in my ups and downs, I seek chaos with naps.
If only I didn't complain too. I will admit
that I like people who try to avoid the option
of mediocrity, no matter whether they succeed
at it or no. These are my people, these
are my pride.

III.

So that's what I believe. So I say. So it goes.
My grandmother dreamt my grandfather
was chasing her down a hill, him in a
child's little red wagon. My brother drew an
upside down head, held by an inhuman hand.
The head was a light bulb, being placed in a socket.
Must we weigh the suffering to give it meaning…
A child sees his family slaughtered in Darfur.
If one has time to contemplate ills, do they
mean more…is that the point of time…
A woman is stoned to death in Afghanistan.
Is it more about poignancy and depth
of emotion…are feelings the thing…
Does it depend on the person, the situation,
and what exactly is our responsibility
in the face of it? Complacency is unacceptable.
We know that. And yet…it sets in, takes hold.
All we want is the one thing we can't have…
to make sense of what matters.

About the Author

Amanda J. Bradley is a poet and essayist living in Brooklyn. She recently completed her Ph.D. in English and American Literature at Washington University in St. Louis, specializing in twentieth century poetry. She teaches Composition & Rhetoric and tutors in the Writing Center at Yeshiva University in Washington Heights.

About NYQ Books™

NYQ Books™ was established in 2009 as an imprint of The New York Quarterly Foundation, Inc. Its mission is to augment the *New York Quarterly* poetry magazine by providing an additional venue for poets already published in the magazine. A lifelong dream of NYQ's founding editor, William Packard, NYQ Books™ has been made possible by both growing foundation support and new technology that was not available during William Packard's lifetime. We are proud to present these books to you and hope that you will continue to support The New York Quarterly Foundation, Inc. and our poets and that you will enjoy these other titles from NYQ Books™:

Joanna Crispi	*Soldier in the Grass*
Ira Joe Fisher	*Songs from an Earlier Century*
Ted Jonathan	*Bones and Jokes*
Fred Yannantuono	*A Boilermaker for the Lady*
Sanford Fraser	*Tourist*
Grace Zabriskie	*Poems*

Please visit our website for these and other titles:

www.nyqbooks.org

www.ingramcontent.com/pod-product-compliance
Lightning Source LLC
LaVergne TN
LVHW011430080426
835512LV00005B/354